# Contents

>>> **e-guidelines** 11

e-le
with

**Yola J**

**n**iace
promoting adult learning

THE COLLEGE OF WEST ANGLIA

**niace**
promoting adult learning

©2007 National Institute of Adult Continuing Education
(England and Wales)

21 De Montfort Street
Leicester
LE1 7GE

Company registration no. 2603322
Charity registration no. 1002775

NIACE has a broad remit to promote lifelong learning opportunities
for adults. NIACE works to develop increased participation in
education and training, particularly for those who do not have easy
access because of class, gender, age, race, language and culture,
learning difficulties or disabilities, or insufficient financial resources.

You can find NIACE online at www.niace.org.uk

Cataloguing in Publication Data
A CIP record of this title is available from the British Library


Designed and typeset by Book Production Services, London
Printed and bound in the UK by Latimer Trend
ISBN: 978 1 86201 319 3

371.92

# Acknowledgements

Thanks to the projects and individuals who have provided material and case studies for these guidelines: The Atmospherics Trust, Buckinghamshire Adult Education, The City Literary Institute, Community Education Lewisham, Carterton Adult Learning, East Northants & Wellingborough Adult Learning Service, Leicestershire Adult Learning Service, North Somerset Council, The Rix Centre, Home Farm Trust (HFT), Karten Centre Abingdon, Tendring Adult Community College and Wandsworth Mencap.

Thanks to Viv Berkeley, Alastair Clark, Jan Eldred, Sal McKeowan, Peter Lavender and Orlane Russell for their help and comments on earlier drafts of this publication.

Thanks also to the organisations that have given permission for screenshots of their software/websites to be reproduced. Microsoft product screenshots are reprinted with permission from Microsoft Corporation. The photographs were taken by Sue Parkins and the author.

# 1

# Introduction

The purpose of this e-guideline is to offer practical guidance on the use of Information and Communication Technology (ICT) when working with learners with learning difficulties in adult and community education settings. It offers information and examples of interesting practice which make good use of ICT. Case studies are used to illustrate effective ways of using ICT in teaching as well as to provide information about software and hardware that can facilitate this.

## Background

ICT is all around us, from the mobile phone to the MP3 player to the PC that we may use everyday at work and home. Having access to ICT and the skills to use it has powerful social currency in the world today. Technology increases access to opportunities for work, leisure and learning. For groups of people who are marginalised in society, access to ICT and the opportunities to develop the skills to use it can be an important support for social inclusion.

When working with people with learning difficulties, effective use of ICT in teaching and learning can:

> provide ways for the learner to have more control over their learning environment;

> increase motivation to learn and involvement in different kinds of learning;

> support choice making and communication skills;

> provide opportunities to learn skills for everyday life.

As one tutor commented:

*ICT is a tool and an incentive. Every week we have a success, everybody feels they have achieved something to take home or put in their folder.*

The quote below is from a young man with learning difficulties who was involved in a project that used ICT to support the development of independent travel skills:

*I went to Clapham Junction and took pictures on the camera to put on the computer for the website. I liked taking pictures of the trains; I took pictures of the market. I learnt the numbers of the bus routes.*

*Staff helped me look up things about the camera and learn about the website. We talked about future life. I am getting certificates for the Internet and PowerPoint.*

*I went to do office work. I sign a book because I am a member of staff. I do filing and photocopying. I would like to get a job using computers in an office.*

## Who is this e-guideline for?

This booklet is for tutors teaching in mainstream provision and those working with people with learning difficulties in discrete provision, that is courses specifically for people with learning difficulties. All of the case studies used are examples of discrete provision for people with learning difficulties. During the research for this publication it was found that use of technology with learners with learning difficulties in mainstream provision was rare. However, many aspects of the practice highlighted in the case studies can be transferred to settings where people with learning difficulties are learning in mainstream provision. Therefore, the information provided in this publication is for:

> ICT teachers who want to know more about working with people with learning difficulties:

*My subject is IT but I can see that the learners could get much more out of it if I understood about working with people with learning difficulties.*

> Teachers who have experience of working with people with learning difficulties and want to develop knowledge of ICT and how to use it appropriately in their teaching:

*I regard myself as having average ICT skills; most of what I know has come from trying it and seeing what happens.*

# Who are the learners?

The term 'people with learning difficulties' is used in post-16 education to refer to individuals who have

> *...a general cognitive learning difficulty that affects their ability to learn. In education, the terms currently used to describe learners with cognitive learning difficulties are 'profound and complex learning difficulties', 'severe learning difficulties' and 'moderate or mild learning difficulties'. In social services settings, the term 'learning disabilities' is used.*
>
> *(DfES, 2001)*

The term **learning disabilities** refers to the same group of people as the term **learning difficulties**.

People with learning difficulties may also have other disabilities, physical and sensory. It is important to note that one in three people with learning difficulties also have some kind of sensory impairment (Mental Health Foundation, 2001). Tutors need to take into account the visual and aural dimensions of their teaching methods.

This particular publication does not look at working with learners whose learning support needs are primarily focussed on what are described as 'specific learning difficulties' such as dyslexia. (See *e-guidelines 9: Supporting adult learners with dyslexia: harnessing the power of technology*.)

# Where do the courses take place?

Learners with learning difficulties attend classes in a range of different settings: their local adult and community education centre; at a social services day centre; in a community setting such as a library; or at a voluntary organisation such as a Mencap Gateway club. Many learners are on part-time courses for one or two half days a week. Others may attend more substantial provision; say for three or four days a week.

## Computer Art - a part-time course for people with learning difficulties

The Computer Art class at the City Literary Institute is a weekly two-hour class for people with learning difficulties. In the summer term the class visited a local museum and, using digital cameras, the learners took photos of various exhibits that interested them. The following week learners downloaded their photos into the Adobe Photoshop programme, some by themselves, others with help from the tutor who used a basic pictorial diagram drawn on a board at the front of the class to support learners in this process.

One learner chose an image of an African figure. He chose a tool from the Photoshop programme, in this case a paintbrush, and drew around various outlines in the picture, changing the colours he used. This involved very precise control of the mouse.

Another learner used the cutting out tool on the programme. She went around the edge of the image and 'cut it out' and copied this image into another file. Several copies of this were made and placed on top of each other to give an interesting layering effect.

*Photo of Buddha adapted using Adobe Photoshop*

# What is the structure of the book?

Chapter 2 gives an overview of the context in which people with learning difficulties participate in adult learning and the key principles of good practice when teaching and supporting this group of learners.

Chapter 3 covers various aspects of access to learning for people with learning difficulties and how the use of ICT can support this.

Chapter 4 describes some examples of current interesting practice in the use of ICT with people with learning difficulties to illustrate key principles of good practice.

Chapter 5 provides information on useful resources and publications.

At the end of chapters 2, 3 and 4 the key points covered are summarised as 'Points to consider' and are suggested action points for tutors. At the end of chapter 4 is a list of tips from tutors and managers consulted as part of the research for this publication.

# 2

## Working with people with learning difficulties in adult learning

This section gives an overview of the context in which people with learning difficulties participate in adult learning and the key principles of good practice when teaching and supporting this group of learners. It looks at:

> disabled learners' rights
> working with people with a learning difficulty
> self-advocacy
> partnership working
> working with support workers

### Disabled learners' rights

In 2002 learners with disabilities and learning difficulties gained new rights under the Disability Discrimination Act (DDA) Part 4 which requires education providers to ensure:

> disabled learners are not treated less favourably than other learners for a reason related to their disability;
> they make reasonable adjustments for disabled learners.

Under the DDA Part 4, all staff now have duties in relation to disabled learners. For instance, if a person with learning difficulties joins a mainstream class it will be the tutor's responsibility to ensure the learner is not treated less favourably than other learners because they are disabled and, if needed, any reasonable adjustments are made.

A tutor working in a mainstream setting may need advice and support from colleagues who specialise in working with disabled learners. However, there are some general guidelines that can be followed to support effective practice when working with learners with learning difficulties. The following points provide a brief guide for tutors teaching in mainstream classes:

## Some ways of working with people with a learning difficulty

In planning your work:

- Find out what the learner is interested in and work from this. For instance a learner may want to talk about themselves and their interests. Learners could take pictures of each other and download them on to the computer or search the internet for information about a hobby.

- Do not underestimate the learner. Many people with learning difficulties can achieve real success when tutors are able to discover what they really want to learn.

- Talk to individuals and groups about their past learning experiences, both what has worked and what has failed. There is no point in repeating past failures. Find out what equipment and software has been used previously and how useful this was

- Make sure learning is age-appropriate. All adult learners need to feel that they are not being treated like children and that they are not endlessly repeating things they have done at school. As one ICT tutor working with learners with learning difficulties remarked:

  *Don't buy children's versions, they can cause the students to feel intimidated and insulted.*

- Make learning as practical as possible. Avoid worksheets if you can. You can use a range of materials. Multimedia tools can introduce visual and audio elements to teaching and learning for example by using an interactive whiteboard.

- Find ways to raise the status of learning – for example many people who have found writing difficult may feel very differently about it if they can begin to use a computer rather than pen and paper.

- If learners have difficulties with concentrating, plan lessons so that there are a variety of short activities.

In class:

- Always explain things clearly and check that they have been understood. Get the learners to repeat back in their own words if necessary. This rehearsal and repetition can help to fix ideas in their minds.

- Be careful not to be too directive; some learners can feel overwhelmed and become nervous.

- Be a good listener. Some people with learning difficulties may say what they think you want to hear. Listen for the underlying meaning too.

- When people have difficulties with remembering things, work with them on creating strategies which they feel might help them to remember. This might include repetition, drawing pictures or using photographs.

- Encourage all learners in the group to ask for help so that this is seen as an important part of learning and not a sign of failure.

- Help learners to record progress and successes, maybe by using pictures and sound rather than words.

Adapted from DfES (2003)

Details of information and publications about the DDA and post-16 education are available from the Learning and Skills Network website: **http://www.lsneducation.org.uk**

## Practical examples using ICT

Do not underestimate learners' abilities. Many centres work on the theme of self and create life stories using PowerPoint. One learner from a centre run by the national charity Home Farm Trust (HFT) has traced her family history with the help of a volunteer. She used the Internet and found that she has some very illustrious and well-travelled ancestors who came from Holland and lived in the West Indies.

Use interactive whiteboards to supplement practical activities. For example, sorting the washing can be a team game using Smartboard software.

Words may not be enough. Use video clips and photographs to support assessment for learners and to record achievement. One centre in Wiltshire encourages learners to use images to build a portfolio of 'Needs, Wants and Aspirations' so that learners can track their own progress.

The TATE project (Through Assistive Technology To Employment) has an equal opportunities policy to help disabled learners to be aware of their rights. This is in symbol form to help everyone understand and remember what it says.

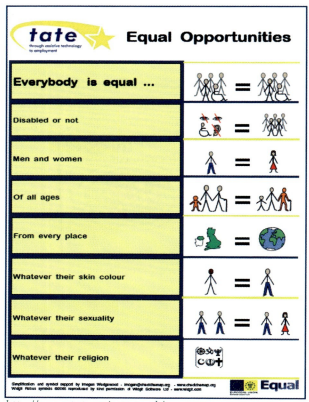

*http://www.tateproject.org.uk/*

# Self-advocacy

Self-advocacy is about speaking up for yourself, making choices and decisions and having your say. Many people with learning difficulties find it quite a challenge to do this, having previously not had many opportunities to speak up for themselves or be listened to and taken seriously. Therefore, a learner may also be developing self-advocacy skills alongside the subject skill. It is important to take this into account as a factor that could influence:

> how you assess an individual's ICT skills. For instance, in the case of initial assessment setting a series of practical tasks and observing over a period of time how a new learner gets on will complement an initial assessment interview in which the learner may find it hard to speak up.

> the choice of appropriate teaching methods and support strategies – building in plenty of opportunities for making clear, uncomplicated choices to increase confidence. For instance choosing between one or two tools in a particular computer programme or the size and type of font they want to use.

> the pace at which a learner will learn – some learners may be slow to hit the switch that activates the computer programme, but this may be due to issues of confidence rather than physical or cognitive ability.

ICT can be a powerful practical tool to support the development of self-advocacy skills. For instance, learners in a self-advocacy class used video when they were discussing different kinds of communication, such as body language and facial expressions, as a learner explained:

*...we video learners interviewing each other. Then we watch the video and commented on posture and eye contact. You can tell a lot about how they are feeling from this.*

*(DfES, 2001)*

ICT can provide ways for people who don't have verbal skills to communicate and speak up for themselves.

## ICT supporting communication

Davinder is a learner in an ESOL group for Asian women who have learning difficulties. She occasionally says a word but mainly uses Makaton signs **(http://www.makaton.org)** and Widgit symbols **(http://www.widgit.com)** to communicate during the sessions.

A Bigmack Communicator switch was introduced to the group, which can record short phrases that are played back when the large switch is hit. Using the switch, Davinder was able to communicate with another learner in the group who is blind and unable to see the signs that she uses. This came about when Davinder was using the Makaton sign in one session for 'What is your address?' The phrase was recorded on to the switch. The blind learner was told that Davinder was going to ask her a question. Davinder hit the switch and the recorded question played.

The tutor feels that using the switch is a good way of reinforcing language and communication with Davinder:

> *She understands well and likes to communicate and be part of the discussion.*

The group plans to use the switch to record their voices and listen to how they sound when they speak.

The tutor found the switch very easy and straightforward to use. There is an on/off button and a record button on the back and

> *What it has over a tape-recorder is that you just have to hit the switch again and it plays back instantly, you don't have to wait for it to re-wind.*

For more information on self-advocacy and people with learning difficulties see:

*The Self-Advocacy Action Pack* (DfES, 2001)
*Our Right to Learn* (NIACE, 2000)
*Self-Advocacy and Adults with Learning Difficulties* (NIACE, 1993)

## Working in partnership

Multi-agency collaboration between education, health, social services and voluntary organisations is key to providing access to education for people with learning difficulties. Many individuals will have a number of agencies involved in supporting them in different areas of their lives. For instance, they may live in supported housing run by the health authority, attend a social services day centre and go to an adult education class. Many centres are now using a new website called Check the Map to find useful services and events (http://www.checkthemap.org.uk)

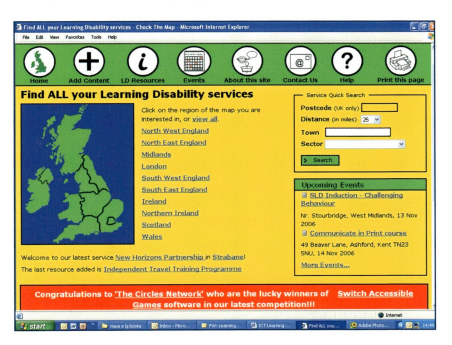

Joint working between different organisations at a strategic level can offer the pooling and sharing of resources, useful sharing of information and 'joined up thinking' and planning.

### Lewisham Computer Project

Community Education in Lewisham run classes for disabled learners that are jointly funded by the Local Authority and the Learning and Skills Council (LSC). A communication class for learners with profound and multiple learning difficulties is one of a number of classes that are part of the Computer Project for people with learning difficulties. Learners use adapted equipment and work with specialised software to develop their communication skills. The Speech and Language team from the local Primary Care Trust (PCT) will come in if requested to help assess and identify the best support for individual learners.

At an individual level, joint working can offer valuable continuity of support for a learner.

### Continuity of support – choosing the right equipment

In the lead up to Christmas one learner was very excited about the fact that he was going to get a new computer. A joint meeting between the learner, his ICT tutor and his residential key worker was held to discuss which computer equipment and software would suit his needs.

## Working with support workers

One of the most important contributory factors that help make a class a good learning experience is effective support for the learner. Many people with learning difficulties will attend classes with a support worker from a day or residential service. The support in class may be from staff, from the learning support team or, as in one case, volunteers helping in a beginners' computer class, which meant the tutor could focus on technical support when it was needed.

It is important that the right kind of support is given in a way that enables rather than prevents the learner from participating and learning. As one tutor commented:

*People who support people to do things often support them to do the 'right thing', rather than choose what they want to do. There tends to be a lot of intervention. You need to wait and respond when they do it.*

As support staff play such a key role in enabling people with learning difficulties access learning, tutor liaison with support staff is essential. In the case of ICT there should be guidance for the support staff if they are to be able to support a learner with specific tasks. One tutor explained how she works with support staff:

*I issue my own guidelines to the support workers on their very first session on the course ... basically outline issues such as help students but don't take over; encourage students to have a go but don't let them get frustrated; ask for help or clarification if unsure.*

*I also find having Individual Learning Plans for each project helps, as support workers then know which skills I would like the students to perform (eventually) unaided and which ones they can give a hand if frustration sets in.*

# A learner support system

In the communication class for learners with profound and multiple learning difficulties at Lewisham Community Education, learners have 1:1 and in some cases 2:1 support. The support workers are given a sheet that specifies the learners' goals for a session mapped to the *Adult Pre-Entry Curriculum Framework for Literacy and Numeracy* (DfES, 2002). The support worker uses this during the class to make notes and completes it at the end of the session after a brief discussion with the tutor.

| Computer project learner record<br><br>SAMPLE | Learner Name: Paul Collins<br>Date: 25/5/06 |
|---|---|
| **Programmes used today** | Disco, Switch it, Patterns |
| **General comments**<br><br>e.g.<br>• preferences<br>• engagement levels<br>• positive interactions<br>• any difficulties?<br><br><br><br>•      Break time | Attempted to use the keyboard before we set up his switch.<br><br>Pictures selected:<br>(1) Parrott<br>(2) Fishing     } Disco<br>(3) Thunder and lightning<br><br>– used switch with patterns programme, unprompted, but with a few minutes rest in between.<br><br>– does not look at the screen unless prompted to, but enjoys the music and sound effects. |

*Continued on next page*

| Goals | |
|---|---|
| | (Sample Goal)<br><br>**Curriculum Element**: Context for Communication and Number<br><br>**Milestone Element**: 1a –1b ( from the Adult Pre-Entry Curriculum Framework for Literacy and Numeracy)<br><br>*Activates a switch using an accidental reflex action.*<br>**HOW**: *The support worker demonstrates repeatedly that the learner's particular movement will trigger the stimulus.*<br><br>*Focuses attention briefly on people (e.g. support worker, other learners)*<br><br>*Focuses attention briefly on events (or objects) such as the computer screen/music, or grasping objects briefly when they are placed in his hand or lap.* |

Form filled in by: Susan Wood. Support worker.

Other learners may have less intensive and instrumental support than the examples given above. In some cases support may be temporary until an individual learner feels confident enough to be in the class on their own. Whatever the level of support provided, there are some good practice points when considering the role of support workers in class. The support worker should:

> sit next to the learner they are supporting so they can offer immediate help when necessary – for instance, pointing to the screen to show the learner where to go next;

> help the learner customise the computer and change the settings if necessary;

> take part in the class activity to help motivate the learner through their involvement and participation – to support the learner to take the picture on the digital camera, the support worker could offer to be the subject;

> encourage the learner to listen to the tutor when appropriate;

> facilitate choice and decision-making at every opportunity, from trying out and choosing the most appropriate piece of adaptive technology to deciding which music sample to download from the web;

> always ask if the learner wants help, they may just want time to consider or complete a task;

> work with the learner to identify the most helpful ways of offering practical support by:
  • breaking down tasks
  • demonstrating how the task is to be done
  • re-arranging furniture or equipment to suit the learner
  • offer physical and visual prompts;

> be positive about the learner's work and achievements;

> encourage the learner to address the tutor and other learners on their own behalf.

For more ideas on the role of the support worker go to **http://www.sflqi.org.uk**, click on 'online material', then click on the Continuing Professional Development Modules, and finally onto the PECF modules. The guidelines are included in session four of the level four module – meeting individual needs.

# Working with people with learning difficulties in adult learning

## Points to consider

Do you need to develop your awareness of the implications of the Disability Discrimination Act and new rights for disabled learners? Who can support you to do this?

What can you do to ensure the use of ICT in your sessions provides appropriate opportunities for:

> choice and decision making
> speaking up and communication

How can you build in time to liaise with support staff to develop effective joint-working strategies?

Can you provide support workers with lesson plans and details of ways they can support learners in particular tasks?

# 3

# ICT and access to learning

This section looks at the role ICT can play in developing fully inclusive learning opportunities by supporting and enhancing practice that improves access to learning for learners with learning difficulties. It looks at access in its widest sense and starts with how information and materials can be made accessible through the use of:

> clear accessible language
> illustrations and other visual cues
> symbols
> multimedia

The section continues by looking at:

> Microsoft accessibility options
> multimedia and access to learning
> icons and accessibility
> accessible facilities

## Making information and materials accessible

Information and teaching materials used in adult learning are primarily produced in text form whether on paper or online.

Language used in education is often specialist and uses jargon. For instance, information about courses, class notes or instructions may only be available in text form and use words such as 'curriculum', *'Skills for Life'* or 'humanities'. This can exclude people with learning difficulties who may need help with comprehending language or who have little or no literacy skills. As one woman with learning difficulties commented:

> *A lot of people don't know what the word 'jargon' means. Say 'we will not use any complicated words, that we do not understand.' The word 'jargon' is jargon itself.*
>
> *DfES, 2001b*

Text can present a real barrier to learning and to accessing key parts of the whole learning experience. Careful thought needs to be given to how text, or indeed any visual materials, can be presented in an accessible form. Given that one in three people with learning difficulties are also likely to have some kind of sensory impairment, standard printed text will be difficult to see. Think about using larger fonts, different colour combinations or a mixture of text and symbols.

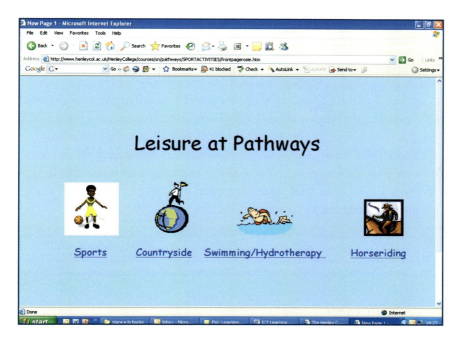

Tutors always have a set of objectives but often these are not shared with learners in a way they understand. Many people benefit from having an overview of a course or project so they can work out where they are, remember what they have done and see what else they will be working on.

## Accessible text

Each learner will have different and varied needs but there are some basic rules that can be followed that help make text easy to read:

> Use a large, clear font – point 14 should be the minimum size used.

> Use short sentences which contain one main point.

> Present text in short sections.

> When preparing accessible text, consult with learners. Ask if the language is clear and easy to understand and if the text is presented in a format that makes it easy to see. Show them a first draft or invite them to be involved in the process from the start.

> Language needs to be clear and free of jargon, e.g. a recent document sent out by NIACE was provided in two versions.

> At the end of a piece of text provide a wordbank that explains any difficult words that it has been necessary to include.

> Writing can also be made easier by the use of wordbanks. Learners working in catering can benefit from having an onscreen personal dictionary of relevant words. WordBar from Crick software has many grids and it is quick and easy for tutors to make their own, geared to a learner's needs and interests. Learners can hear the word by right clicking on it and can insert the word with a left click. This speeds up composition and gets round some spelling problems.

| café | cake | catering | cheese | chef |
| chill | chop | chopping board | coffee | cold room |
| cook | cooker | cooler | course | cutlery |

## Making text accessible

**Standard version of text**

Learning also contributes to community wellbeing, cultural creativity and social solidarity – in ways that can be quantified.

**Accessible version**

Learning for adults is not just about getting a job, it also helps people to get out and make friends, learn about things that they enjoy and are interested in, and learn skills to get on in life.

Extract from *The Big Conversation* (NIACE, 2006)

Pictures from CHANGE Picture Bank

The website **http://www.easyinfo.org.uk** provides guides on how to make information accessible to people with learning difficulties. It includes a guide on how to present computer-based information in a way that is clear and easy to understand. The site lists useful resources and tools that can be used; provides links to organisations that specialise in making information accessible; and shows examples of this work.

# Illustrations and other visual cues

There are a number of ways adult learning staff produce accessible information and teaching materials. Placing pictures, illustrations and photos alongside text helps reinforce the meaning. It is important to match the most appropriate picture to the corresponding text and not to use too many pictures on one page. A resource frequently used for this is the CHANGE picture bank. This comes in the form of a CD-ROM and is available to buy from **http://www.changepeople.co.uk**.

Pictures can be a great help. They can motivate and add value by making print more attractive and professional looking. They can stimulate thinking. They can help to explain written content, remind the reader of key concepts and give cues. Illustrations may provide a broad context into which words fit. For example, a price list in a café may be easier to read if there are pictures of sandwiches against the word 'sandwiches'.

Clip art and photos can also be used. Take care when using clip art as images depicting disabled people can be of variable quality. One useful resource available on DVD or CD that uses positive photographic images of disabled people is Photosymbols: **http://www.photosymbols.com**

Tutors and learners can use their own photos taken with a digital camera and insert them into a word-processed document. Alternatively, they may like to create photo stories using the free software Photo Story 3 for Windows. This produces very professional mini videos but the value lies in the process – talking, planning, making choices – as much as in the final product.

## Symbols

Symbols are used alongside text or to replace text entirely. Two systems frequently used are Widgit Rebus symbols and Makaton. Many special schools use these symbol systems and consequently some, but by no means all, learners may already be familiar with them by the time they are an adult learner. The Widgit website, **http://www.widgit.com**, provides information and resources for children and also adults. The Makaton Language Development Project gives information about Makaton symbols and resources and can be found online at **http://www.makaton.org**.

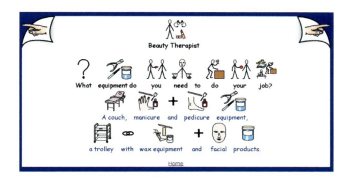

It is worth bearing in mind however, that Widgit and Makaton symbols create a system that has to be learnt and decoded/translated by the individual in order to be understood. It will not be a universal system/language known to everyone and will therefore exclude those who don't 'speak' this language.

## Widgit Rebus Symbols

At the City Literacy Institute, tutor Duncan James has used Widgit symbols for the words for a song sung in the World Music class for students with learning difficulties:

*I use Widgit … in this case I used very large and bold symbols with tiny words to show how I found the symbol (trial and error, often not the original word of the text).*

I like to rise when the sun she rises
Early in the morning
And I like to hear them small birds singing
Merrily upon their layland
And hurrah for the life of a country boy
And to ramble in the new mown hay

Widgit Rebus symbols used with permission from Widgit software

# Multimedia and accessible information

Audio versions of text can be particularly helpful to individuals who have limited or no vision. This can also be an additional support for those learners who can see, as they can listen to an audio version of text and look at the accessible document. For instance, if you want to consult with your learners using a questionnaire approach, prepare an easy to read set of questions with supporting illustrations or photos. Make an audio recording of the questions, perhaps asking a learner to record the questions onto an MP3 player, which allows easy and unobtrusive recordings of the voice. Learners can record their responses too. Using free software, such as *Audacity*, it is easy to edit sound recordings so learners can have their hesitations edited out.

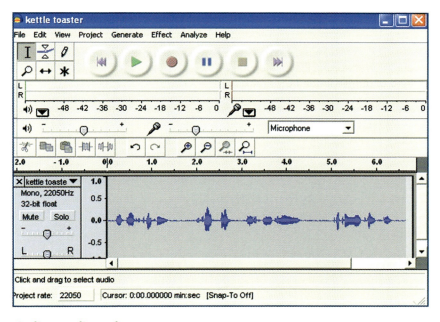

*Audio recording software*

## Inclusive learning materials

*Training for Change* is a training pack for people with learning difficulties who want to be involved in training as trainers. It was produced by NIACE and Change (a national organisation run by disabled people that campaigns and works for equal rights for all people with learning disabilities, including those who are also deaf or blind).

In order to make the *Training for Change* pack fully accessible to all people with learning difficulties the pack is produced in the following formats:

- A folder with printed course notes written in accessible language with illustrations
- An audio version of the text that people can listen to as they follow the illustrated text
- Accompanying video material that uses British Sign Language signing throughout

There is more information on the use of ICT when working with deaf learners in *e-guidelines 10: Using technology to promote inclusive education for adults with hearing impairments.*

## Microsoft accessibility options

Microsoft provides an accessibility option that can be used to adapt the various functions of Windows programs. This can be found by going to the Control Panel in My Computer and clicking on Accessibility Options. There are options for users who have visual impairments, hearing difficulties and limited mobility.

A key resource that explains these accessibility options is 'Benevolent Bill - What Microsoft does for Accessibility'. This gives details of the range of accessibility features available in Windows and Word. It can be downloaded from the TechDis website at:
**http://www.techdis.ac.uk/**

# Using accessibility options with learners with learning difficulties

Rebecca Keane, a tutor at Carterton Adult Learning, teaches an IT Workshop for Beginners. This is an entry level course for learners with severe learning difficulties where each learner has a support worker working with them in the class. The emphasis of the course in on:

*...using IT as a means to communicate, by using a multimedia and visual approach, instead of the more traditional text based one.*

Rebecca uses various methods and accessibility options to support learners to use the keyboard and mouse and make the cursor easier to see.

*If the learner finds it hard to double click, I teach them to right click then choose 'Open', which is usually the first option on the drop-down menu.*

*I use Control Panel / Accessibility / Keyboard (tab) for the following:*

- *If they press too hard on the keyboard keys so that the same letter is repeated many times, I set FilterKeys option so it slows repeated keystroke.*
- *If it is difficult for a learner to depress two keys simultaneously, I set StickyKeys option so they can press one key after another*
- *If the learner is partially sighted or has difficulty pointing to icons accurately on the desktop, I set Control Panel / Display / Appearance (tab) to Windows Extra Large.*

*As an alternative to highlighting text in Word by dragging across I teach the learner to left click at start of text then use Shift key and directional arrow keys (up, down, left, right) on keyboard to highlight the text. You can of course use the stickykeys option so they just press one key at a time.*

*All the instructions to do this are given to the support worker who makes the adjustments for the learner each time they come to class and resets it at the end. It is not something I expect learners to be able to do without support.*

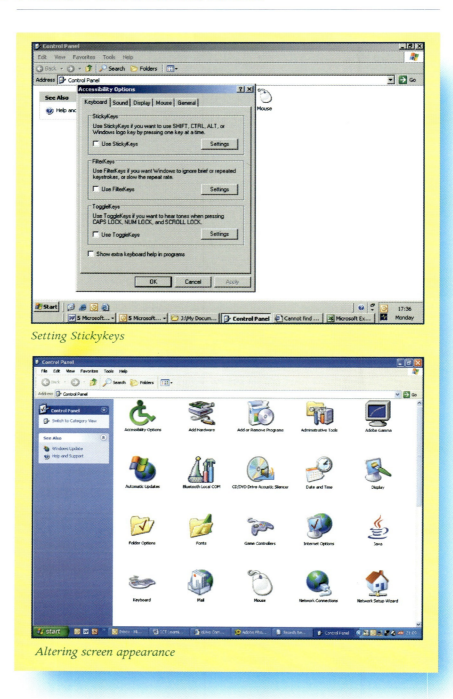

*Setting Stickykeys*

*Altering screen appearance*

# Icons and accessibility

The standard icons system featured on Microsoft Word toolbars can be used and adapted to support learners with limited literacy skills. A variety of methods can be used to help with learning and remembering their meaning. (Reading icons is a literacy skill in itself and can be mapped to the *Adult Pre-Entry Curriculum Framework for Literacy and Numeracy*.)

## Icon recognition

In the Introduction to Computing class at the City Literary Institute, tutor Orlane Russell reinforces icon recognition by drawing the icon on a chart or card and an enlarged image of the icon can be projected onto an interactive whiteboard. Orlane makes a point of describing the appearance of the icons to the learners as they are learning to use them:

*Click on the red cross to close …if you want to copy, it is the two sheets on top of each other.*

Another technique used in this class to help recognise the different functions in Word menus is to encourage the learner to look for first letter repetition of a command rather than the whole word:

*The menu board can be too wordy for some learners. Some look for F for File and as there is only one F this works as they can often recognise by the first letter. 'New, Open, Save' can be learnt as a system. E.g. 'File' recognise the first letter, shape of the word, where it is on screen. 'Exit' – remember it is the last word on the list. These are all literacy cues.*

# Assistive technology

There is a vast array of computer equipment available that can support disabled learners to access ICT. ICT classes that take place in computer suites in adult and community settings have the advantage of a specific location to store this equipment. However, unless support is available to help staff learn how to set up this equipment it can stay in its package in the cupboard and not be used. It is important to try things out and see what works best for an individual. Get advice from others who work with the learners at the centre.

The case study below is a good example of how support to access ICT can be provided in an outreach location through the use of relatively simple but effective means.

## Outreach support using assistive technology

Eve, who is in her late eighties, attends an Introduction to Computers course at her residential home. The course is run by the local Adult and Community Learning (ACL) provider. Eve has poor eyesight and was struggling to use the laptop as the keys were too small for her to see.

The ACL Inclusive Learning Manager visited the class and sat with Eve. She took with her a keyboard with overlays (in this instance, intellikeys). She simply plugged the large keyboard into the port on the laptop; this allowed Eve to access the large keyboard. The keyboard came with overlays. The overlay that Eve preferred was the keyboard that set the letters out in alphabetical order and not the QWERTY system that is normal on PC's. This entailed no additional training on the part of the manager as the overlays configured themselves.

The Inclusive Learning Manager also changed the colours on the screen to maximise visibility for Eve. In Eve's case she preferred yellow font on a black background. This was easily achieved through the accessibility option in the control panel.

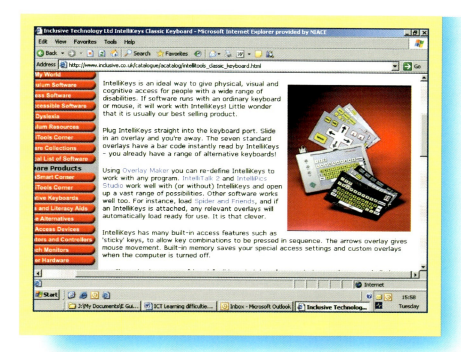

A useful website is AbilityNet, a charity that produces information on resources and techniques that can be used to support disabled children and adults in their use of computer technology (**http://www.abilitynet.org.uk**). They have produced a CD-ROM, *Successful Computing for Disabled People*, which gives details of hardware and software available to enable people with physical and sensory disabilities to use computer technology. There is also information on resources to support people with reading and writing difficulties. It includes video clips of equipment being used and fact sheets on how to adapt various bits of equipment, for example 'Keyboard and Mouse Alternatives'.

Inclusive Technology (**http://www.inclusive.co.uk**) supplies assistive technology, as does Ablenet (**http://www.ablenetinc.com/**). One of the most useful devices has been the touch monitor, as the HFT Karten CTEC centre reports:

*The touch monitor's brilliant for the people we work with because they don't have to have the cognitive understanding that doing something on a keyboard has a reaction on the screen. You can just go straight to the screen and get the cause and effect.*

33

## Assistive technology to support learners with profound and multiple learning difficulties

In the Communication class at Lewisham, one learner, who has very restricted use and control of his arms, uses a lever attached to a bracket on his wheelchair, which, when moved, activates the computer programme he is working on. He is working with a programme that displays a large coloured pattern on the monitor. Each time the switch is hit by the learner a further section of the pattern appears on the monitor.

Another learner in this class uses two large switches, one red and one yellow. Images of the red or yellow switches are shown on the monitor and flash on the screen and the learner chooses the matching switch to build up a simple image. In the picture below the learner is using an overlay keyboard which uses symbols.

## Accessible facilities

Access is most frequently used to refer to the physical environment. There are a number of key things that will help make a room where computers are being used accessible to disabled learners, such as ramped access for wheelchair users, plenty of room to move around in, and height-adjustable tables for easy access to the computer. For people with learning difficulties the rules for accessible text will apply to any signs that are used as directions to the room or notices in the room. The video *How to be Accessible: The Top Five Things You Need to Know* (Ufi-Learndirect) highlights areas that need to be considered including:

> providing enough room around computers for any adaptive software;

> having chairs available that are secure and do not move;

> listing any adaptive software and hardware available, ensuring a member of staff knows how to set up the hardware and software.

## ICT and access to learning

### Points to consider

> What existing ICT resources available to you could be used to develop accessible text, e.g. clip art, digital photos, advice from learners with learning difficulties?

> Could this work be incorporated as part of the ICT curriculum you are teaching?

> Could any of the Microsoft accessibility options usefully support your learners?

> How can you customise standard features of programmes, such as icons, to improve access for learners with learning difficulties who don't read?

> Are there sources of advice available in your organisation or with partner organisations on assistive technology and its use?

> Could you carry out an accessibility audit of your ICT facilities with disabled learners?

# 4

## ICT and learners with learning difficulties

Developing ICT skills may be the primary focus of a course, as in an Introduction to Computing class; it can be a tool for developing creative skills where learners are composing music by mixing samples and soundtracks on the computer; a tool to support inclusion for new learners coming to college; or to help communication.

This section examines examples of practice that illustrate the use of ICT:

> when using person-centred approaches to learning;
> in learning that is based on the learner's strengths and interests;
> that supports the learning in different ways and at different paces;
> to develop life skills;
> to support learning in real life contexts;
> to help respect learner choice on participation;
> to help choice, decision-making and increasing independence.

### Person-centred learning and ICT

The term person-centred planning is commonly used in the context of services for people with learning difficulties, particularly since the publication of the Department of Health White Paper *Valuing People* (2001), a strategy for services for people with learning difficulties in the twenty-first century. **http://www.valuingpeople.gov.uk**

Person-centred planning is a planning process that places the individual at the centre and focuses on what is important to them from their own perspective. The principle of person-centred planning has clear overlap with those of *Inclusive Learning* (FEFC, 1996), which recognises the importance of matching learning to individual needs.

Post-16 education is developing person-centred approaches to work with people with learning difficulties by listening to what individuals want to learn and developing learning programmes to help them achieve their goals.

A person-centred approach to planning courses means involving learners at all stages in the planning and teaching process. This will ensure that the learning experience will be relevant to the needs of the individual and that they will be motivated to learn.

## Negotiating the curriculum

Tutor Rebecca Keane plans her Beginners Introduction to IT course by placing the needs and wishes of the learners at the core of the planning process:

*At the start of the year, we spent the first session discussing the course content. Previous assessments from myself and the tutor before me enabled me to plan beforehand an outline of generic skills students might like, e.g. word processing. I drew up a draft programme plan and syllabus and we went through this in the first session. I described this in terms of activities rather than ICT skills.*

*Students then told me additional activities they would like, some being repeats of the previous year and some new ones. I then mapped the activities to the skills I would like them to learn. The students like to talk about themselves, so I planned lots of activities to give them that opportunity. The students were getting quite 'comfortable' using certain software so we discussed using other software, e.g. Internet, digital photography and web page creation. I demonstrated some of these before we made up our minds.*

Audio recordings of what learners have to say about what they want to learn can provide a very direct and person-centred approach to the planning and assessment of their learning. Text and paper-based materials can be inaccessible for some learners with learning difficulties. The use of ICT tools can help move away from this reliance on text.

## Using ICT to recognise and record achievement and progress

Tutors working for East Northants and Wellingborough Adult Learning Service are using MP3 players in a variety of ways to support their work with learners with learning difficulties.

At the start of their courses, learners, using the MP3 players, record their own learning goals. Amanda Clarke, Curriculum Manager (Supported Learning) explained:

> This is a way for all verbal learners at any milestone to say in their own words what they would like from the course. The targets are written down on the Record of Work/Learner Target Sheets. This is especially good if it is someone else who is assessing the learner and gives the information to the tutor. It is also good for assessing and asking what additional needs are required for the higher milestones.

Recording the learner's voice in this way can also be used as an ongoing form of assessment. The same process is carried out at the end of a course or session and is saved to voice file for the learner's evidence as part of the RARPA process.

At the start of the year a member of the E-Learning team came to a Supported Learning meeting to give a 45-minute demonstration session on how to use MP3 players. Tutors are now familiar with recording, downloading to a PC and burning a recording to a CD. Amanda Clark commented:

> Anybody who is fairly computer literate will find it easy. If you can use a memory stick then you will be able to use an MP3 player.

It is important to get an MP3 player with a voice recording function that has a good capacity for memory as each recording will use a lot of megabytes.

Video and webcams rather than written reports can be used to record events, case conferences, and so on, and develop real person-centred planning.

The Karten Centre in Abingdon uses a person-centred approach. As part of this, service users are helped to record their life stories using a range of multimedia tools. Scanning photos, using voice clips and choosing how to present work helps participants recall and value memories. Family, friends, carers and employers may all have photographs, letters or other memorabilia to contribute.

## Learning based on learners' strengths and interests

Many people with learning difficulties have had negative experiences of education and learning. Therefore focusing on what they find difficult and can not do can be very de-motivating and can provoke strong psychological barriers to learning. Concentrating on what learners can do and their interests will help to provide a positive response to learning and will motivate the individual.

### ICT and music making

Music Lab is a class that runs at Lewisham Community Education for people with learning difficulties. The class is run by two tutors who are experts in working with computer technology and are great music enthusiasts. Most, but not all of the eight learners, attend the class with support workers. The aim of the class is that by the end of the year learners will all have their own CD of music they have composed in the class and learnt how to burn to a CD.

Learners download sound samples of favourite film music from websites – for example the James Bond theme tune. The samples are put into folders and inserted in a programme called Reason. Learners use keyboards and can add their own music to the samples. Tutors support the learners to choose sounds that they like – for example, one learner liked heavy drums, so appropriate samples were found for him to choose from.

Learners listen to each other's work at the end of the session and comment. The tutor explains how the music was developed by breaking it down into the steps that the learner followed, with the learner joining in with their own comments.

The EJAY dance manual programme is used. It has a very visual interface and learners can drag and drop samples into a time line. Programmes can be used at different levels of complexity.

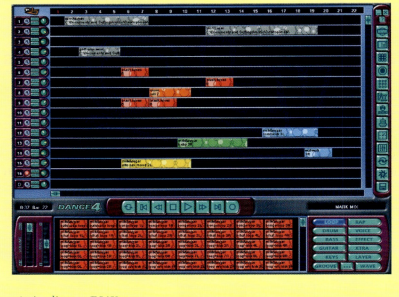

*A timeline on EJAY*

## Learning in different ways and at different paces

ICT can be a key tool in supporting flexible and person-centred teaching approaches. Many learners with learning difficulties will have quite marked spiky profiles, that is they will have some strong skills but other skills may be much less well developed. One example of this could be an individual whose verbal skills are not strong and rarely talks, but who understands most of what is said during a class and can follow instructions with minimal support.

The example below illustrates how ICT has supported an individual who has difficulties with socialising to be included in learning activities.

## ICT and distance learning

A course supporting people with learning difficulties to access college allowed learners to work extensively with multimedia resources in their sessions, developing PowerPoint presentation about themselves, their lives and interests. One learner, who is autistic and has barriers to meeting new people, found it very difficult to attend the sessions. The work that the group had covered was burnt to CD and sent to this learner. A key worker helped the learner with this process and sent the responses back to the tutor. This was an ongoing process for a number of sessions.

Differentiating activities during sessions is key to meeting the needs of learners learning in the same class at different paces. Differentiation is built-in to some specialist software such as SwitchIt Patterns, used in the Communication class at Community Education Lewisham. This programme builds up a picture on the screen by using a system of cause and effect – the learner hits the switch and part of the pattern appears. At the most basic level this can be done in one step, at an intermediate level three steps, and at an advanced level five steps.

## Differentiation in ICT activities

In the Computer Art class at the City Literary Institute, most learners will learn how to use three tools in the Adobe Photoshop palette such as the:

> Marquee tool – this draws regular shapes and fills them in.

> Magnifier tool – this is good for detailed work to help with vision and mouse control.

> Lasso tool – this can be used for cutting and pasting parts of images which can then be saved separately and used for repeat pattern design.

The tutor has modified the programme to make it easier by reducing the number of choices on the tool bar. As learners learn at different paces the tutor can respond by gradually introducing more tools once a learner is ready to move on.

Recognition of icons is also taught at different levels in this class, to best suit the range of skills-development of the learners. This has been broken into three levels:

> Read and match

> Speak and match

> Point and match on the screen

## Multimedia

Multimedia tools can be used very effectively in sensory learning situations with learners who have profound and multiple learning difficulties. The skilful use of visual and audio stimuli produced by multimedia tools can be very engaging for learners who need a lot of support with communication and interaction.

### Using multimedia to support communication

North Somerset Council Lifelong Learning Team worked in partnership with The Atmospherics Trust to deliver a course to learners with profound and complex learning difficulties. The aim of the course was to enable learners to develop their communication skills, group and social skills and concentration skills.

The Atmospherics Trust uses a sensory integration programme that combines colour, images, music, smells and tactile materials. It is designed to provide a rich sensory environment to stimulate the brain's sensory processes. **http://www.atmospherics.org.uk**

A data projector and laptop were used to provide moving images. During the sessions specifically designed DVDs were run showing a particular timed colour sequence. Sounds and music were played on a CD player, and a camcorder and digital camera were used to record the learners at work and gather evidence to show progression. One tutor remarked:

> ...Although it took a few weeks, we were beginning to see definite anticipatory responses. People were engaged by the changes of colour and picture, and waiting for it to change. This was mostly observed in changes in facial expression, ceasing or beginning of rocking, and vocal people became quiet.

When working with multimedia, the immediacy of the cause and effect of touching a key or switch and activating a sound can be very rewarding for learners who most of the time have very little power over their surroundings.

The pace of learning in such situations will be very gradual but the significance of small and subtle responses of learners with complex needs can be huge. Such responses can indicate significant achievements in learning. Capturing and recording this progress is key to supporting the individual's learning.

## Tracking progress in multimedia-supported learning

At a day centre some of the learners with profound and multiple learning difficulties had responded to a music-making machine which was like a small electric organ. The sound was started and controlled by breaking a light beam. You could select the type of music it made. This enabled people with very limited movement to use the machine, so long as the light beam is directed accurately at the part of the body the learner is best able to use. In the case of one of the learners, it was her eyelid.

The practitioners could see the learners:

> understood that the music started and stopped in response to their movements, i.e. cause and effect;

> could indicate the type of sound they preferred;

> were enjoying themselves.

These responses were in themselves something of a breakthrough for individuals who generally show limited response to their environment. With time, they noticed that the learners were making real progress in terms of:

> motivation

> concentration span

> control of their movements

They wanted to be able to measure and record this success, but did not know how to do so. By looking in the *Pre Entry Curriculum Framework* (PECF) at the Contexts for Number, they found that the activities matched with:

Milestone 2a.3 – Accept and engage in explorations
M 2a.5 – React to new experiences, by purposefully committing their attention to an activity or change in activity
M 2b.4 – Communicate consistent preferences and affective responses
M 2b.5 – Remember learned responses over short periods of time
M 3a.4 – Explore materials in more varied ways
M 3b.4 – Actively explore objects and events for more extended periods

The practitioners concerned had not previously seen a connection between what their learners were achieving through the use of ICT and literacy or numeracy. They were delighted to have a formal way to describe the achievements, and to monitor progress in a systematic way.

## Life skills and ICT

As with all learners, those with learning difficulties want learning to be purposeful and to learn skills that are relevant to their lives. This could be to help them get a job, learn how to read and write, or travel independently. Many people with learning difficulties want to work. There are of course a range of skills needed to do any job and the use of ICT in teaching and learning on a vocational course for people with learning difficulties can help develop these skills.

## The development of ICT skills on vocational courses

Learners with learning difficulties on the OCN-accredited Workskills course at Tendring Adult Community College in Essex, decided that they wanted to develop a webpage to go online via the college website. The content of the page was based on their own interests, jobs and hobbies. Learners discussed what they wanted to go on the webpage, typed up their ideas using the symbol system Widgit and edited their work after comments from other learners.

During this process the learners learnt how to scan photos, use digital cameras, search the internet and input clip art into Word documents. The class tutor commented that the learners:

*...developed all sorts of different skills; literacy; communication and making choices. For a couple of learners their mouse control really improved, this was a lot to do with the fact that they were working on things that they are really interested in.*

## ICT supporting travel skills

Wandsworth Mencap worked with a group of learners to engage them with community travel through e-learning. The learners recorded their journeys using digital cameras. This material was then downloaded and learners were supported to edit their material, design their own websites and then present their work to other learners. The learners worked in a computer suite at the day centre. Sessions were led by a tutor and learners worked with support workers and volunteers.

Equipment used included computers with large-key keyboards, editing software and a backlit whiteboard. The advantage of a backlit whiteboard is that you don't get shadows falling across the screen. FrontPage software was used to develop the webpages. One of the staff involved in running the project commented:

*If one is not creative enough, technology can be too heavy for the person. You have to make it relevant to them.*

# ICT and learning in real life contexts

Learning in real life contexts is particularly important for people with learning difficulties. Individuals may have been socially excluded from many situations and therefore not had the chance to develop certain skills. Practical real life situations are immediate and make it easier for the learner to understand the relevance of the skills that they are learning.

Video and photos make it much easier to focus on real and everyday things in learning. They can be instantly available on computer screens by searching the net or using the image search option on Google.

## ICT and learning in real life contexts

Tutor Maggie Jones at Northamptonshire Adult Learning Service teaches on the Preparing for Work course for adults with learning difficulties. Katie, one of the learners on the course, recorded her experience of learning office skills using a PowerPoint presentation. Photos and sound were added, as Maggie explained:

*With Katie's PowerPoint I did a session like an interview and asked Katie questions, which I taped on the MP3 player. Katie typed her words on the slides and we inserted the sound clips together.*

*I used an MP3 player for the first time this year. I have found that the instructions can be very off putting and often the actual process is quite easy. It was surprisingly easy to do and I think the learners enjoyed listening to themselves.*

PowerPoint is frequently used as a means of presenting learners' life stories, work done in a class and individual learning plans. It can incorporate sound, photos, video, illustrations, text and symbols. You can use all of these options or just some depending on what is most appropriate for the learner. The flexibility of this programme means it can be used by and with learners with a wide range of abilities, skills and interests. Learners can be taught how to put together their presentation and if they choose to, how to present their own work in this form. This can be a particularly empowering experience.

A new guidance document, *Person-Centred Approaches and Adults with Learning Difficulties* (DfES, 2006), provides a CD which looks at how to produce learning plans using PowerPoint. It gives hints and tips on using Word and PowerPoint and integrating photos and video clips.

## Respecting learner choice and participation

The skilled use of multimedia can enable great flexibility and individualism in learning. It can offer a range of ways learners can participate in learning, whether directly involved in an activity or watching from the sides.

### Multimedia supporting different levels of learner participation

Working in partnership with two local authorities, the City Literary Institute runs a course to support people with learning difficulties who have not attended college and want to do so. All learners attend with support workers.

During the session learners can choose to do various activities based around the use of multimedia tools. A laptop is connected to a large interactive screen or Smartboard. A small camera (that can be directed to individual learners working at a table facing the screen) projects their live image on to the screen. A number of devices activate the camera: a small musical keyboard as well as a couple of large switches. The learners choose which piece of equipment they want to use. The screen is the focal point of the session.

One learner chose not to participate or sit with the group but to watch the screen. She was regularly encouraged to join in but her wish to stay physically outside of the group and watch the screen was respected. This itself is considerable progress as previously she had found it difficult to stay in the classroom at all.

## Helping choice, decision-making and increasing independence

For some people with learning difficulties, coming to a centre to attend a class and be in a group with others can be a huge challenge. Technology, if effectively used, can provide opportunities for more choice in the way people can learn. Crucially, for people with learning difficulties it can provide more control over their learning and how they learn.

### Developing confidence in the learning experience with ICT

Learning Together is a class for people with complex needs who are new to working in a group and coming to college. After one and a half terms, the group started work on a video about coming to college. Members of the group drew their own storyboard and made a video recording of this. Learners then chose which part of the video they wanted to make.

The support worker for one learner drew a bus and talked to the learner about her journey to college. They filmed her journey starting with a shot of her travel card, her bus journey and the short walk to the college. Her goals for the class were to:

> be relaxed in college

> have experience with interacting with others

> choose a subject in the class

Another quiet learner filmed different parts of the college: toilets, canteen and learners using the lifts. Once the filming was complete the group edited the video.

The programme used was 'imovie', which the tutor described as 'very intuitive'. It gives a timeline and puts clips in different boxes – learners can then drag them down to where they want them to be in the timeline. Voice recording or music can be added.

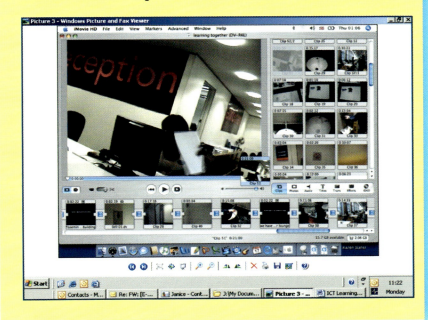

## Conclusion

The case studies featured in this e-guideline illustrate a range of ways that ICT is being taught and used in adult and community learning provision with learners with learning difficulties. They all have at their core a strong positive approach to working with people with learning difficulties and the use of ICT is correspondingly appropriate and effective.

A final example of this is of a certificate created by a learner with learning difficulties. He was encouraged by the tutor to use many of the skills he had learnt on his course when designing his certificate. The certificate celebrates his achievements and records his future plans for learning ICT skills.

*Carterton Adult Learning*

*Well Done to*

**Martin Walker**

*You finished a 30 week*

*Computing For Beginners Course*

*Things you did really well*

*Made a calendar.*
*Made a poster using clip art and word art.*
*Changed the font type.*
*Working on your own.*

**THINGS FOR YOU TO GET BETTER**

Using powerpoint
Using E mail
listening to other people
Using two hands to type

Signed: _____     Date: _____
Rebecca Keene, ICT Tutor

Signed: _____     Date: _____
Lisa McIntyre, Development Worker

Signed: _____     Date: _____
Lynn Dowler, Widening Participation Manager (N)

# ICT and learners with learning difficulties

## Points to consider

> What can you do to put learners' interests, choices and aspirations at the centre of your planning and recording achievement and progress, and how can ICT help?

> How can the flexibility and adaptability of ICT be used to support learners who learn in different ways and at different paces?

> How can ICT be effectively embedded into teaching that supports the development of life skills?

> How can you use ICT to enhance learning in real life contexts?

> How can you use ICT to support teaching that provides a range of options and levels of engagement for learners who are just starting to participate in formal learning settings?

# Tutor tips

Below is a collection of hints and tip from tutors who use ICT in their work with students with learning difficulties:

## Literacy and ICT

*Encourage students with developing literacy to access clip art to support their writing.*

*You don't need to be able to read complete menus to access them, students can remember that exit is at the bottom of the file menu, and use first letters and icons to access other options.*

*There is a basic skills element to the work, for instance wanting to do typing. Use things that the students can relate to. They dictate to me so they can then type up their own words.*

## Accessibility

*Key commands can be great shortcuts and lessen the need for mouse control. For instance Control+S for save and Control+B for bold.*

*Use Google image to get instant pictures of subjects you are discussing.*

*Expand on the menu and desktop metaphors; do they help students access the computer interface?*

*In Photoshop it is good to use a full screen mode as it has less information and you loose the menu bar so can't click on it accidentally and exit image.*

## Planning and teaching

*Don't set targets too high. It is important that there is individual negotiation to make each session achievable and have steady progression. It's about individual learning and setting individual targets.*

*If you use a variety of approaches and methods people get a chance to shine at different things.*

*Make sure you keep on taking digital images of the learners at intervals so that you have got a good resource bank of pictures to choose from for PowerPoint presentations of their work.*

*I always prepare examples to show students before we embark on a unit, e.g. I prepared a PowerPoint presentation about me before students did theirs. I did the same for the website. This really helped them see what they are asked to achieve. Having a Smartboard really helps for demonstration purposes.*

*Recognise the importance of students learning from each other.*

## Staff support

*A large number of staff are terrified of technology, but are getting better. Most things need clear short instructions (with pictures) written up for tutors otherwise they won't use them.*

# 5

# Resources and websites

This section provides information about:

> some commonly used ICT equipment
> internet sites that are designed to be accessible
> some useful websites

## Equipment

### Digital cameras

Learners at Wandsworth Mencap used Digital Blue Cameras, which they found robust and easy to use. A practitioner suggested the following checklist when looking for a digital camera to buy. The camera needs to:

> be sturdy
> be value for money
> have a high storage for memory
> have an internal memory card
> have a good battery life
> have a rechargeable battery – which is key
> produce good quality pictures
> be easy to turn on and off

For further information on using digital cameras in teaching see *e-guidelines 2*: *Digital cameras in teaching and learning*.

## Interactive whiteboards or smartboards

Interactive whiteboards or smartboards can be used for a variety of purposes. The image from a computer screen is projected onto a large interactive screen. This provides a good focus for learners and can be particularly helpful for visually impaired learners. It is good for tactile learning as learners touch the screen to activate the functions of the program. It can also be used very effectively for demonstrations. As Lyn McDermot from Leicestershire Adult Learning Service commented:

> *Learners really focus on what is going on... They are superb for accessing visual materials quickly. For instance, a holiday venue comes up as part of a discussion, a quick trawl through Google and all the learners can see the topic.*

> *Smartboards are fantastic when linked to the 'Millionaire' voting system. Fabulous for 'fun' assessment activities and very interactive. Has a serious purpose as assessments can be recorded and printed off to support folder work, RARPA etc., but gets away from 'yet another worksheet' syndrome.*

### Using the 'Millionaire' voting programme for learner evaluation

The 'Millionaire' voting system is an interactive programme where people can vote. This has been used with learners with learning difficulties for course and activity evaluation purposes.

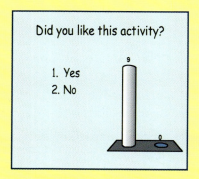

Did you like this activity?

1. Yes
2. No

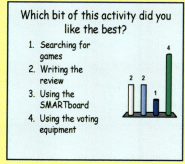

Which bit of this activity did you like the best?

1. Searching for games
2. Writing the review
3. Using the SMARTboard
4. Using the voting equipment

## Photo printers

Photo printers print off photos directly from the digital camera so there is no need to access a computer. Leicestershire Adult Learning Service uses photo printers with learners as they can print the photos they have taken as part of the session. The printers are quite portable but expensive to run so unless they are used by learners in a lesson tutors will do any other printing on a computer.

# Internet

## Myguide – easy access to the Internet

The Department for Education and Skills has launched a website which aims to provide a 'radically simple' way of using the Internet. The website is aimed at people who have, in the past, avoided using the Internet. Because of this many people 'miss out on the many economic, employment and social opportunities' that using the Internet can bring, not to mention learning opportunities.

Myguide will be useful to all learners but especially those with sensory impairments, physical disabilities, learning difficulties and older people. Myguide is free. A click of the mouse will enable the user to change the interface to make it more accessible in terms of colour and font size. Additionally, a click of the mouse will enable the user to 'hear' the page being read to them. The clutter free approach to the website makes it user friendly and far less frightening to navigate.

Some reading skills are required and the 'hear' facility can support those who have difficulty in accessing text. Teachers can use Myguide in a number of ways with learners, e.g. supporting learners in setting up their own email accounts. The search engine facility is also easy to navigate and can be used for learners to conduct their own research in a self directed manner, as appropriate. Less teacher support means more learner autonomy.

Visit **http://www.myguide.gov.uk** for further information.

## Project @pple

Project @pple was a research project carried out by the Rix Centre at the University of East London. The aim of Project @pple was to explore how people with learning disabilities access and participate in e-learning and the World Wide Web. The project has developed a learning environment for 'personalised learning with an e-portfolio feature to enable multimedia authoring for self-advocacy and assisted communication'. For further information see **http://www.rixcentre.org**

## The Big Tree: an Internet portal for learning disability

The Rix Centre has launched an online portal designed to be accessible to people with learning disabilities called The Big Tree. It provides links to websites of interest to people with learning disabilities and their supporters, guidance on the use of the internet and multimedia, news about The Big Tree, accessible articles and information. Visit **http://www.thebigtree.org**

# Websites

**http://www.abilitynet.org.uk**
AbilityNet helps disabled adults and children use computers and the Internet by adapting and adjusting their ICT.

**http://www.aclearn.net**
Advice om using ICT with learners.

**http://www.drc.org.uk**
*PAS 78 Guide to good practice in commissioning accessible websites*
This guidance document is aimed at those responsible for commissioning or maintaining websites and web-based services accessible to the public. The DRC found that 81 per cent of British websites are inaccessible to disabled people, despite the fact that since October 1999 website owners have a legal duty under the DDA to ensure that services provided via the web are accessible to disabled people. The guidance is available free from the DRC website.

**http://www.easyinfo.org.uk**
A website about making information easier for people with learning difficulties. Easyinfo.org.uk is for everyone working with people with learning difficulties and for people with learning difficulties themselves.

**http://ferl.becta.org.uk/**
FERL is an advice and guidance service supporting individuals and organisations in using ILT within the post-compulsory education sector. There is a focus area on adults with severe learning difficulties that looks at teaching and learning and provides information, case studies, and suggestions for activities.

**http://www.hft.org.uk/**
Home Farm Trust is a charity which supports peple with learning difficulties.

http://www.inclusive.co.uk
Suppliers of educational software, switches and computer access
devices, simple communication aids and assistive technology.

http://www.makaton.org
Makaton is a unique language programme offering a structured,
multi-modal approach, using signs and symbols, for the teaching of
communication, language and literacy skills for people with
communication and learning difficulties.

http://www.techdis.ac.uk
TechDis Works is an educational advisory service, working across the
UK in the fields of accessibility and inclusion. TechDis aims to
enhance provision for disabled students and staff in higher, further
and specialist education and adult and community learning through
the use of technology. TechDis provides information and advice,
resources for technology related to disability and inclusion, and staff
development within the context of technologies and disability. Details
of the Microsoft accessibility options are available on this website
when you search for 'Benevolent Bill'.

http://www.valuingpeople.gov.uk
Valuing People is the Government's plan for making the lives of
people with learning disabilities and their families better. The website
has information on what Valuing People is about and how it is
currently being implemented. This site has been made accessible for
people with learning difficulties.

http://www.widgit.com
Website for widgit software.

# 6

# Glossary

| | |
|---|---|
| **Discrete courses** | Courses that are for a specific group of learners. In the context referred to these are courses for people with learning difficulties. |
| **Google** | A popular search engine. |
| **IT** | Information Technology. |
| **ICT** | Information and Communication Technology. Technology incorporating networking and computers. |
| **ILT** | Information and Learning Technology. Supporting and delivering effective learning through the application of IT and ICT. |
| **Internet** | The worldwide network of computers. The terms Internet, net, World Wide Web and web are often used interchangeably, although technically the web is a subset of the Internet. |
| **Mainstream courses** | Courses that are open to all adult learners. |
| **MP3 player** | A digital audio player. |
| **Multimedia** | Used to describe the inclusion of graphics, sound and videos to enhance learning materials. |

| | |
|---|---|
| **PowerPoint** | A popular presentation graphic programme, part of the Microsoft Office suite. |
| **Adult Pre-Entry Curriculum Framework (PECF) for Adult Literacy and Numeracy** | A framework that covers literacy and numeracy for adult learners at pre-entry level. |
| **RARPA** | Recognising and recording progress and achievement in non-accredited learning, an approach which applies a staged process to recognising and recording progress and achievement in learning. |
| **Self-advocacy** | People with learning difficulties speaking for themselves and making their own choices and decisions. |
| **Valuing People** | The Department of Health White Paper published in 2001 that sets out a strategy for services for people with learning disabilities in the twenty-first century. |
| **Widgit** | A software company specialising in symbol software, projects and resources. **http://www.widgit.com/** |

# 7
## Further reading

DfES (2001a) *Access for All: Guidance on Making the Adult Literacy and Numeracy Core Curricula Accessible*, London: DfES

DfES (2001b) *The Self-Advocacy Action Pack*, London: DfES

DfES (2002) *The Adult Pre-Entry Curriculum Framework for Literacy and Numeracy*, London: DfES

DfES (2003) *New Rights To Learn: A Tutor Guide to Teaching Adults After the Disability Discrimination Act part 4 July 2003*, Leicester: NIACE, http://www.niace.org.uk/research/HDE/documents.htm

DfES (2006) *Person-centred Approaches and Adults with Learning Difficulties*. London: DfES

DH (2001) *Valuing People*, A White Paper, London: TSO

Jacobson, Y. (2000) *Our Right to Learn*, Leicester,: NIACE

Mental Health Foundation (2001) *The Fundamental Facts*, London: Mental Health Foundation

NIACE (2006) *The Big Conversation*, Leicester: NIACE

Sutcliffe, J. and Simons, K. (1993) *Self-Advocacy and Adults with Learning Difficulties*, Leicester: NIACE

Sutcliffe, J. in collaboration with CHANGE (1998) *Training for Change*, Leicester: NIACE

Taylor, N. and Chacksfield, J. (2005) *ICT for Learners with Special Needs: A Handbook for Tutors*, London: David Fulton